The Homeschooling Mothers Bible Study:
God's Encouragment for Homeschooling Mothers

by Jan L. Burt

The Homeschooling Mother's Bible Study
Copyright 2005 by Jan L. Burt
All rights reserved. No part of this book may be reproduced or transmitted in any form or by any means without written permission of the author.
NIV used unless other wise noted

ISBN:

Godly Encouragement for Homeschooling Mothers
5021 Pembrook Court
Wichita, KS 67220
www.AllThingsHomeschool.weebly.com
www.MomsWhoHomeschool.blogspot.com

Cover image designed at Canva.com by Jan L. Burt

2

Table of Contents

- How To Use this Book — p.4
- Introduction — p.5
- Week One — p.6
- Week Two — p.17
- Week Three — p.29
- Week Four — p.39
- Week Five — p.54
- Week Six — p.68
- Notes — p.81
- Memory Verses — p.82
- Daily Bible Reading — p.84
- Recommended Reading List — p.87
- Re-Order Form — p.89

How to Use This Book

I would like to take a few moments to address the use of this Bible study. I highly recommend memorizing the verses each week. This is foundational to our continued growth in the Lord. I also suggest utilizing the Daily Bible Reading List included at the rear of your book. You will be blessed to spend time in God's Word on a regular basis, and the completion of the daily reading will aid you in getting the utmost from this study. The Recommended Reading List is a compilation of some of my favorite books, although for the sake of space I did not add nearly ALL of my favorites. It is a good mix of books, giving the reader some nice choices for a variety of tastes and topics. Finally, I have included an order form page. If you enjoy this study, feel free to pass on the ordering information to a friend. You can also use this information if you would like to contact me. I intend to write future studies aimed at homeschooling mothers, so feel free to contact me in regard to ordering my future publications.

Now I would like to address the daily studies. Each week contains five lessons. You may complete the lessons on any day of the week. For example, you need not do your lessons Monday through Friday. If Sunday through Thursday works best for you, use that schedule. If you prefer to work at your own pace, allowing yourself the option of taking a day off mid-week, that would work as well. Of course if you should decide to use this study in a group setting, you would need to have your lessons completed on time for your weekly meetings. You could also spread the lessons out over 12 weeks, although I advise against taking too long to complete a short study like this one. When you have the option of delaying something, it becomes very easily placed upon the back burner. The effectiveness of the study would be lessened by these delays as well. The lessons are short, in keeping with our roles as women who homeschool. I felt that lengthy lessons with plenty of daily work could become burdensome, considering the type of schedule most homeschoolers keep. I hope I have achieved at least some of what I set out to accomplish. May you be blessed by the Lord as you continue to grow in faith and train up your children in the way they should go. Thank you for allowing me to be a part of your homeschool journey.

The Homeschooling Mother Bible Study Introduction

Though there are numerous articles, e-newsletters, magazines, websites, books, support groups, and co-ops for homeschoolers, and though there are dozens of Bible studies and study tools, groups, etc. for homeschooled children, there is a large void in the area of Bible studies written specifically for homeschooling mothers.

So after much conviction from the Lord, I am writing one! It may be used alone or in a group setting. It can be done at the user's own pace, although lessons should be completed weekly. Of course, time with the Lord on a daily basis is the best encouragement for homeschool mothers, and prayer is essential for any Bible study to succeed!

The bulk of my experiences as a homeschool mom are probably not much different than most homeschoolers – multi-tasking, several children, living on one income, lack of space, lack of time, lack of energy, financial strains, extra-curricular activities, etc.

A few of my experiences are probably very different than some of my fellow homeschoolers. Children with learning disabilities, physical disabilities, health problems, familial strains, a son with a serious heart condition, trials and struggles in various areas of life that seem at times unending, (I have a dear friend who regularly asks me upon answering my telephone call, "What happened now?"), a husband in the military along with his full time job and continuing education, friends that have gone to war, etc.

So, if by the wide expanse of experiences I've been through – both prior to my acceptance of Christ as Savior, and after that glorious event – I can encourage even one homeschool mom in her day to day weariness, then I can truly say all I've been though has been worth it.

Week One

When the Lord planned the works He desired each of us to accomplish as His children, He also had plans to prepare each of us accordingly! While that sounds lovely enough, we soon come to the realization that the work He has planned for us is hard and beyond our own abilities. The preparation is often like a military boot camp, while we might prefer a 2-day conference where we learn all we need to know about our ministry in seven climate-controlled sessions, with prepared outlines! Take comfort if you find yourself ill equipped to be a homeschooling mother. That's a safe place to be! The Lord uses weak and fear-filled people to do His will (Moses, Gideon, and Esther come quickly to mind), and as Paul said, when we are weak, then we are strong.

Day One

Let's begin our study of God's word by looking in Ephesians chapter 3. Please read verses 1-6, carefully focusing on verse 6. Here we read that, as Gentile believers, we have an equal share in all the riches inherited by God's children, and that we enjoy the promise of blessings through Christ Jesus.

So, what does that have to do with the day to day tedium of a homeschool mom's life? Everything!! We have an equal share in God's riches, and we enjoy the promise of blessings. We have great resources at our disposal, ladies! So let's utilize all that God has for us!

Take a moment to write down your biggest areas of difficulty – these can be issues that just "popped up" today or ones you've been dealing with for years. Either way, God can handle them! There isn't anything that needs fixing that He lacks the tool to repair! List these concerns below, and take some time to pray over them, giving them to Jesus to "fix".

_____
_____
_____
_____
_____
_____
_____

Now, as these problems come to mind again (whether they are hand-delivered by the enemy or are simply in your way all day and you can't escape them) remember that you share in the riches God doles out, and you enjoy the promise of blessings from Jesus. Do you think that there is anything you listed above that God's riches or Jesus' blessings cannot alleviate? Praise His holy name; there will never be anything that He can't "fix"! Amen!

So, in the course of your homeschool day, please recall to mind that in giving your "fix-it list" to the Lord and then pressing on in the ministry that God has given you (namely homeschooling your child/children), that is how you best serve Him in that moment. Don't let Satan steal one more blessed day with your children from you! Give God your worries, and rest in the knowledge that if he desires to involve you in the "repair" process, He will surely let you know! But God can accept the fact that you do not intend to let your school day come to a grinding halt over the list of concerns you have already handed over to Him.

Day Two

Yesterday we began by reading in Ephesians chapter 3. Let's continue there, looking first at verse 12. Let the words soak down deep into your heart. These are some powerful words! My translation, the New Living Translation, reads this way; "Because of Christ and our faith in Him, we can now come fearlessly into God's presence, assured of His glad welcome." Now that is a verse to memorize!

This verse doesn't give a lengthy list of conditions; it merely gives one. We MUST have faith in Christ (our personal salvation). If you know Christ as your Lord and Savior, having accepted His atonement for your sin, then you have met the requirements to believe God for the promise of this verse.

Fellow homeschooling mothers, we have all had days when the last thing we are able to give is a "glad welcome". We can't always say we are totally loving toward our children, our friends, our husbands. But the Lord CAN say that! In fact, He promises it! Just as if we have been away from home for an extended time, our Abba Father wants us to be assured of His glad welcome. This is news we need to engrave upon our hearts, lest we ever forget His great love for us. When is the last time you entered your prayer time assured of His glad welcome? If you can't recall, you're not alone! Trust me on this one, if there was no discouragement within the Christian community there wouldn't be so many publications, support groups, seminars, and even conventions! No, you are not alone in your discouragement and weariness – but you also are not LEFT ALONE to cope!

Today I would like you to prayerfully write down some reasons why you may not feel God's "glad welcome" during your personal prayer time. Perhaps you simply never thought about your prayer time in this way before, but for some of us there may be deeper issues that need to be tended to. Let the Loving Father tend to your heart now, and evermore be assured that you are gladly welcomed!!

_____
_____
_____
_____
_____
_____

Now, in order to secure this assurance into our hearts and minds, we need to do exactly what we would tell our homeschooled children to do – memorize this verse! We do not home educate our kids so that they can try to fight the enemy without any weapons. We desire to equip them, to enable them to stand strong in these dark days. We also need to be well equipped, because as long as we draw breath, our time spent in battle is not ended. And our Helper has not yet finished with us.

So, our first memory verse is Ephesians 3:12. Choose any translation you wish. Some people can easily memorize the King James Version, while others prefer more recent translations. Whichever you decide to use is fine, so long as you memorize it! It is absolutely NEVER a poor use of time to hide God's Word in our hearts. It is always deadly, however, to attempt to go into battle with no weapons in our arsenals.

Practice several times each day, keep your verses on note cards to review frequently, put the verse to music – work at it diligently, because this Living Word is the only thing that will truly enable us to persevere and succeed in our homeschool endeavors.

Day Three

Let's begin today's study right in God's word. Please read Ephesians 3:14-20. Once again, we are reading some power packed verses! There is a wealth of priceless encouragement in today's reading, but I will try to hone in on some key verses that are very relevant to us as homeschoolers.

Verse 14 beautifully describes God's plan, meaning His all encompassing plan of Redemption. In the NLT this verse reads, "When I think of the wisdom and scope of God's plan, I fall to my knees and pray to the Father."

If I could, I'd like to put a new spin on this verse. We need wisdom to plan, purchase, implement, and execute each homeschool year; one might say we need a scope and sequence of sorts. It aids us in having a clear vision for each homeschool year. This verse addresses both the "wisdom" and the "scope" that we so desperately require. The answer to our need is contained in the remainder of verse 14, to fall on our knees and pray to the Father.

Now, homeschooling is obviously not what Paul was writing about to the church in Ephesus! However, I sincerely believe that God's Word can speak to us in any situation. So long as we are not blaspheming the Lord or misusing His Word I believe it is acceptable to Him to encourage one another with Scripture. God be praised!

Next, let's look over verse 16 and see what we can glean from it. This is a verse that can change our lives if we really allow it to penetrate our hearts. We see that God has glorious and unlimited resources that He uses to dole out mighty inner strength to us through His Holy Spirit. Notice this strength will bring Him glory as it works itself out in our lives. These resources have absolutely no limit! I don't know about you, but there isn't a single thing that happens in the course of my day that can stretch beyond limitless, mighty strength!

Let's pause here, but before ending today's brief study in the Word, take a moment to write out which of these verses most touches you at this stage in your life. Allow God to minister to you right now. Please consider writing down your thoughts and perhaps even what God speaks to your heart. This is just between you and the Lord, for no one else to see, but it can be a great source of encouragement to look back and reflect upon the things that the Lord has revealed to you in the past. May the Lord richly bless you on this day.

A Verse That Spoke to You: _____

_____
_____
_____
_____
_____
_____

My Time with God:

Day Four

Yesterday we read Ephesians 3:14-20, and focused on just a couple of verses. Today let's focus solely on verse 20. Once again, we have discovered another terrific memory verse for us as homeschoolers! When we take God's Word into our lives by means of memorization, we are acting in faith that His promises are true. It is an act of living faith to store up this treasure in our hearts, and we know that our Father rewards our faith and credits it to us as righteousness (see Romans chapter 4). These are more than adequate reasons to memorize God's Word, and Ephesians 3:20 is a great verse to store up in our hearts. Please write it out on the lines below.

_____
_____
_____
_____
_____
_____

The first portion of verse 20 says, "Now glory be to God!" Have you ever considered the fact that you are a part of a select, chosen generation? God's Word proclaims it to be so. Think about that for a moment; let it ruminate in your heart and mind. Those of us who homeschool as a direct result of a call from God are a part of something big. No, something HUGE!! We have reason to say, along with Paul, "Now glory be to God!"

Please take a moment here to write down a few things that you can thank God for.

_____
_____
_____
_____
_____
_____

Whatever you wrote down, it is worth giving glory to God about. He deserves it, and we ought to give it. In your prayer time today, please thank and praise Him for the things listed above. I am thanking and praising Him for you.

The latter portion of Ephesians 3:20 reads this way in the NLT, "By His mighty power at work within us, He is able to accomplish infinitely more than we would ever dare to ask or hope." Again we see that His mighty power is at work in us, assuring us over and over that there will never be a task, situation, relationship, emergency, or homeschool day that is beyond His power that is already inside of us! (It reminds me of those commercials with the bunny banging on his drum, with the power source on the inside. That isn't a unique marketing scheme; it's as old as God's Word!)

This is a great verse to commit to memory for many reasons, one of those reasons being that it is an easy verse to pray at stressful moments during the school day. I am known to pray for "exceedingly, abundantly above and beyond all I can think, ask or imagine" about almost anything! Try praying this verse and others throughout the day, and see if you don't find yourself drawing closer to the Lord as you communicate with Him more and more often.

Now, I'd like to get to the meaty part of the lesson. This verse tells us that He is able to complete infinitely more than we could ever dare to ask or hope. What power is contained in those few words!

Let's take note of the use of the word "infinitely". Can you count to infinity? Some of your littlest math students might think they can count to no end, but we know better! So here we have the assurance that the God who called us to homeschool our children can accomplish (or complete) more than infinity in their lives! That pretty much covers any concerns we might have in regard to state curriculum standards or recommended reading lists. What an encouragement God's Word is to me!

You get to dig into the rest of verse 20 now. It speaks about God doing more than we would ever dare to ask or hope. I have listed several translations of this verse below. Reading them over, please write down exactly how this verse relates to your life as a homeschooling mother. What hopes do you have for your children, for yourself? What dreams are there hidden in your heart that you may not have asked God for? Are there things you desire to see accomplished in your life and in your children's lives that you have barely even hoped for, let alone spoken aloud to anyone? Have you ever whispered those things to the Lord?

Take stock today, and dig deep, fellow homeschoolers! Write it down in black and white – don't wait any longer to begin to let God fulfill your hopes and dreams!

> "And to Him who is able to do exceedingly abundantly what we ask or think, according to the power that is working in us," YLT

> "Now to Him who is able to do exceedingly abundantly above all we ask or think, according to the power that works in us," NKJV

> "Now to Him who is able to do far more abundantly beyond all that we ask or think, according to the power that works within us," NASB

> "Now unto Him that is able to do exceeding abundantly above all that we ask or think, according to the power that worketh in us," KJV

"Now to Him who is able to do above and beyond all that we ask or think, according to the power that works in you" HCSB

"Now glory be to God! By His mighty power at work within us, He is able to accomplish infinitely more than we would ever dare to ask or hope." NLT

Praise the Lord; He is so much more than merely able to accomplish all those hopes and dreams, ladies! He is better than any knight is shining armor we might ever find on this old earth! He is God!!!

Day Five

We have spent the first four days of this week in the third chapter of Ephesians. While this is a passage with a wealth of encouragement for us as homeschooling women, today we are going to move on to a different portion of Scripture. Please open your Bible to Mark 13.

Before we begin today's look into God's Word, I'd like to take a moment to pray.

Father, thank You that You care so deeply about each woman reading this study. May You pour out Your love upon each one, Lord, and fill them with a passion for You and Your Word. Sustain them as they take on this task You have called them to, and pour Your wisdom out upon them, that they might walk in Your ways as they lead their little ones to You. Bless the time they spend with You, Father, and multiply fruit in their lives. In the precious name of Jesus we pray, AMEN.

Feel free to write out any pressing concerns you may currently have, and expect to receive great comfort from the Word as we look intently at it today.

_____
_____
_____
_____
_____
_____

In Mark 13:28-29 Jesus is speaking of His return to this world. He gives the example of the fig tree beginning to bud. The NLT reads, "Now, learn a lesson from the fig tree. When its buds become tender and its leaves begin to sprout, you know without being told that summer is near. Just so, when you see the events I've described beginning to happen, you can be sure that his return is very near, right at the door."

Several things jump out at me from these verses, but we'll only look at a couple of them for the sake of time. Although I could spend all day digging treasures out of the mine of God's Word, I suspect He might just want me to get up and go live out some of the things He has chosen to teach me!

I love that this translation (the NLT) tells us to "learn a lesson". That is what we work to do all day, all week, all year as parents who home educate our children – we impart lessons to them. Oh how sweet it is when we grasp that the Lord fully understands us! I realize that in this passage Jesus is telling us to watch and be aware of His soon return, to pay attention so we won't be caught unawares. However, I also know that all of God's Word is useful to teach, edify and correct His church, so I believe I can safely glean from this verse (and others) that God fully knows my life situation and struggles, and He completely understands me.

The next point I would like to touch upon is that we need to realize that the buds are sprouting everywhere around us. The summer is nearly here! God has not set us apart as Christian homeschoolers for no good reason. Waste is not a part of God's economy. We are part of a chosen generation, called to undertake this great task in these last days of the earth. I refuse to believe that any of our homeschool efforts are wasted – they will all count for God's glory, because God gets done what He sets out to do!

Be encouraged! You are co-working with God in His long-standing endeavors in the final days in the history of this planet. How can we doubt whether or not God will help us teach higher math or chemistry? Why are we shocked when we feel pressed in upon from all sides? There should not be surprise, as our enemy may more fully realize our task than we do! There should be no doubts as to God's plans for us – ladies, they will all turn out for His great glory!

Let's close this week by reading these two verses again, letting the seriousness and encouragement of what we are REALLY doing fall fresh upon us. Please write out verses 28 and 29 of Mark 13 on the lines below.

Today I haven't left much room for you to study God's Word or answer any questions, so I would like to encourage you to read all of Mark 13 today as a most vivid reminder of the impermanence of this life and the high calling we have as followers of the Lord Jesus Christ. Choose a verse or two that strike you and spend some time in prayer to our Great God, who calls us and equips us for our wonderful calling.

Week Two

Day One

Please open your Bible and read Romans 1:8a. Although our translations may not read exactly word-for-word, the message is clear. The NLT says, "Let me say first of all that your faith in God is becoming known throughout the world." What a beautiful word picture!

Now, just as a reminder, I am aiming to do one main thing via this study – to encourage and edify my fellow homeschooling moms. My "spin" on the verses that I quote is in no way meant to discredit the text into which they were originally penned, and I trust that the Lord accepts my usage of these verses as a means to strengthen the body of Christ. My commentary may not be traditional, but I think we would all agree that ministry comes in many different forms. (See 1 Corinthians 12)

With that said, I would like to focus once again on Romans 1:8. In reference to the homeschool community, there is indeed a similarity I find worth pointing out; we, too, are becoming "known throughout the world". We can relate to that! But more importantly, God can relate to us. He relates to us as we seek Him out and do His will in the manner He so chooses for each of our lives. And I can't help but think that He is pleased as He sees the mark that Christian homeschoolers are leaving on this generation.

The remainder of this verse in Romans reads, "How I thank God through Jesus Christ for each one of you." It must have meant so much to believers in Rome to know that Paul thanked God for them! I can't think of many things that I would treasure more in my heart than to know that someone thanked God for me.

Can I be frank for a moment? Trust me, ladies, even if you have never been told outright that someone is thankful for you, odds are that one day someone will thank you, whether you homeschool one child or ten. There will very likely come a time in each child's life when they will become so aware of what was given unto them that they will thank you. I truly believe that! I believe it because the God I believe in blesses faithfulness – and there is no other faithfulness quite like that of a Christian homeschool mother!

Pause here and make a short list of all the other homeschoolers you know, or simply know of. If you are unaware of any other homeschoolers, then list yourself, and you can list me.

_____
_____

Today, thank the Lord of heaven for whoever is on your list. Let's follow in the example of Paul and thank God for our fellow sojourners!

I would like you to take time today to read all of Romans 1 and 2, writing out any verses that speak to your heart or any insight you glean from His word. Read expecting to receive from the Father today!

My Time with God:

Day Two

Today's verses are two that were in your reading from yesterday; Romans 1:11-12. I would like to focus on verse 11 with regard to our children, and verse 12 with regard to our fellow homeschool moms.

Verse eleven speaks of a desire on the part of Paul to share a spiritual blessing with the church in Rome, the goal being to grow the believers up strong in the Lord. Do you desire your children to be strong in the Lord? Is one of your goals (possibly your primary goal) as a homeschooler to impart spiritual blessings to your children with that end goal in mind?

What do you think some of the "spiritual blessings" were that Paul wished to pass on to his fellow Christians?

_____
_____
_____
_____
_____
_____
_____

What are some of the "spiritual blessings" that you want to pass on as a heritage to your children?

_____
_____
_____
_____
_____
_____
_____

These are the most noble of all your aspirations in homeschooling your child or children. Keep them in mind as you go through each day. In fact, you may want to post these spiritual goals in the room where you teach your children.

Now let's direct our thinking to Romans 1:12. Here we read that Paul was eager to encourage these Christians in their faith. He also desired to be encouraged by their faith. This was a reciprocal arrangement. How often do we gather together as homeschooling women with the intent of encouraging others? I think we may all have such a load upon our shoulders that we feel as if we've achieved something great just by gathering together at all! While there is some truth to that, Paul teaches us something very different.

Now please do not misunderstand me. When I originally wrote this book, I was a homeschooling mother of five, the wife of a husband with two careers and continuing education, no family within 400 miles, and as Director of Children's Ministry in my church (not to mention a desire to be involved in the lives of my neighbors and other friends), I realize that being told you ought to give more of yourself in any area of your life can feel like a death blow. But remember this is not a task you can complete in your own strength. In fact, there is no aspect of homeschooling that I would recommend attempting in your own strength! In essence, what Paul is saying to us is that we should mutually encourage one another. That mutual encouragement has to start with one person doing the encouraging, and it will become contagious from there.

This doesn't have to be a daunting task. Encouragement comes in many forms. A brief note, a sincere "hello", listening intently, laughter, or even sharing openly about a trial or struggle can all be very encouraging. Homeschool moms need to know they are not alone, that they're experiences aren't unique, that others are pressing on and moving forward, even if it is just in small increments! And above all, we need to encourage each other in the Lord, for nothing is impossible with Him.

Please take some time to brainstorm today. Who has God placed in your life that could use some encouragement? I believe we all have at least one such person in our circle of influence, whether or not they homeschool, and whether or not they are a Christian. Write down the names of people who come to mind.

_____
_____
_____
_____
_____
_____

Lastly, today I would like to encourage you to stay connected, both with the church body and the homeschool community. These are two places where encouragement is always needed, and where you can find plenty of encouragement for yourself!

Day Three

Today let's begin in Matthew. Please turn to chapter 5 and read verses 1 – 12. After reading through this portion of the Sermon on the Mount, please write down which of the Beatitudes most speaks to you right now.

_____
_____
_____
_____
_____
_____
_____

I think verse 3 touches me most at this point in my life. The NLT reads, "God blesses those who realize their need for Him, for the kingdom of Heaven is given to them." This is a beautiful picture of salvation. It may take a substantial amount of loss and pain, but it is well worth is if we realize our need for God. And our reward is the kingdom of Heaven, our eternal life. I also draw encouragement from this verse with regard to my homeschool struggles. I am comforted to know that He will be there to aid me as I realize my great need of Him.

There are many areas in which I need to "grow up" spiritually, but a list of just a few would include struggles with health issues of two of my children, a lack of "alone time" in which to prepare and plan for each week's school, and some trials with one of my daughters that manifest themselves in every area of our family life. As I realize my need for Jesus in each of these situations, I truly am blessed, and I am comforted as He aids me.

Now it's your turn. Write out some key areas where you realize your need for God. Turn your needs into a prayer of praise, and request the help you so greatly need.

_____
_____
_____
_____
_____
_____
_____

Let's return to Psalm 71. Please find the second portion of verse 18, and copy it on the lines below.

_____
_____
_____
_____
_____
_____
_____

These words ought to clearly state what our job really is as homeschoolers who are Christians. I want very much to proclaim the Lord's power to this new generation, starting with my children! This is a verse to memorize and then to pray in regard to our ministry to our children. In focusing solely on ourselves spiritually, we may accomplish a few great things for God's glory, but in pouring ourselves into our children, they may well go forth and reach hundreds or thousands of people for God's glory.

Don't misunderstand me on this point. I am thrilled whenever I see women studying God's Word, and I am not advocating anyone placing their own walk with the Lord on the back burner. What I am saying is that it is a wise use of our time to teach our children the ways and Word of God. I not only teach my children at home, but also have taught hundreds of other children in Sunday School and Children's Church classes, Vacation Bible Schools, Pioneer Clubs, homeschool group classes, church nursery groups, Community Bible Study, and more. My experience with the children from Christian homes is not limited, and most of the parents of these children truly love the Lord! Few of them appear to be flippant about their walk with Jesus. Yet there is one disheartening common thread that runs throughout all these groups of children; they simply do not know God's Word! Their minimal grasp of the Bible is often downright shameful. Rare is the child I teach who truly knows God's Word. Many of these kids don't even know the "basics". And while we as homeschoolers may think we're doing a better-than-average job with our own kids (because we truly are!), may I suggest that we ought to aim a whole lot higher?

Here is my reasoning: If all these Christian children and youth are growing up with no real grasp of God's Word, how can they stand once they leave the safety of their Christian home? And if they do manage to stand, what will the cost be? Why in the world do we feel it is somehow acceptable to simply fail to teach our children God's Word?! If these are not yet the last days, then we are rapidly approaching that time. Could it be possible that one HUGE reason God has in the Christian homeschool movement is to raise up a standard among the coming generations? I firmly believe that to be true.

So may I once again challenge you to make your #1 goal in your family school to impart as much of God's Word and His great love to your child or children as you are able. Work at this with great diligence! And remember that God will not waste one ounce of what you teach your children about Him.

Now, it's your turn to write out a list of goals for your children. Don't feel overwhelmed! Start small, writing down some things you truly want to see accomplished in their lives. Then pray about it – ask God to give you His vision for your children. Trust me, He has one! Revise your goals as often as needed. Post them where you can regularly check and see how you're doing. This may be one of the most important things you ever do as a parent because it can so vividly impact your children's futures.

Day Five

Please turn with me to Mark chapter 5 and read verses 21 through 43. There are multiple lessons available to us in this passage of Scripture, but I'd like us to focus today on simply trusting Jesus.

Upon salvation, each of us as Christians trusted in Jesus. But that is different than trusting Him on a daily basis. We need to do both – one secures our salvation and the other gives us continued security until we reach eternity.

In Mark 5 we read about two needy people – Jairus the synagogue ruler and the desperate woman with an illness of some twelve years. We can use both of their experiences with Christ to spring us on toward greater faith and trust in Jesus. Let's start with Jairus.

Although his fellow Jews might not have approved, he boldly came to Jesus in his time of great need. His daughter lay dying, and he forced his way through the throng of people to plead for her to be healed. Ladies, there will be times when we will simply have to press through in our prayer time. And the greater the need, the harder we will need to pray. God is able to do anything, but He always desires to grow our faith. He performs two-fold miracles in this way – changing our situation externally and changing our hearts internally.

In the middle of Jairus's encounter with the Messiah, an ill woman entered the scene. This is a woman who had already trusted greatly in men, and had been terribly disappointed, even taken advantage of by those men. (Please see Mark 5:26) I'd like to take a moment here and touch on a subject that bears some weight among the women of our day.

Some of us were raised in Christian homes, while others of us were not. Either way, we have all been exposed to the feminist push forward in our country over the last several decades. And many of us have been taken advantage of by the men of our society – one of the reasons the feminist movement continues to find success. May I be so bold as to say we could take a lesson from this dear woman in Mark chapter 5? We can see from Scripture that she had previous experience seeking aid from the men in her society – and they appear to have left her without her money, or her health; in fact, the Word of God tells us that she was worse!

Some of us have been worse off after trusting men. But the evidence surrounds us that we are not better off in the hands of other women! We need to do exactly what this dear lady did – pull up our bootstraps, and fight our way to Jesus, spiritually speaking. Destroy those negative thoughts that keep you from reaching out for Him. Dear ladies, He is trustworthy! In fact, Psalm 103 teaches us that he will not treat us as our sins deserve – He is so much more than trustworthy, He is also full of grace and mercy!

I cannot speak for anyone other than myself, but I would love to hear the Lord ask me, "Who touched me?" Oh, to have such faith that in the midst of great activity, the Lord would pause and take note of just me! I can hardly imagine what it was like for our dear sister. Whatever hurts we may have experienced at the hands of others, He is SO worth our trusting Him!

One last lesson from the woman with a hemorrhage. How long had she had this illness?

_____

If you homeschool your children from Kindergarten to their senior year, how many years of teaching will that be?
_____

The correlation here is that He will fill our need every time we reach out for Him, every moment of every day of those twelve years. Let's trust in Him!

Now, back to Jairus and his dying beloved daughter. What does his servant tell him in verse 35?

_____
_____
_____
_____
_____

Although the wording may vary slightly from one translation to another, the impact is still the same; death had come to Jairus' house that day. Now, please read verse 36 and write down Jesus' response to this grim news.

_____
_____
_____
_____
_____

Oh, glory to God! How I love to see in the Word of God that Jesus our Lord ignored the negative comments of the messengers. What an example to us! The Lord Himself will have the LAST say in each and every situation – and we should listen for His words to us and respectfully ignore naysayers and doubt spreaders.

Now please do not misunderstand me on this point – I am not telling you to disregard your physician, your spouse, or your pastor. What I am saying is keep the faith! Keep hope alive – choose not to give in to hopelessness! Let me give you a personal example.

My son has been diagnosed with dysplastic aortic valve and a subsequent ascending aortic aneurysm by a well-known pediatric cardiologist. Basically, one of my son's heart valves is misshapen and does not properly close when the heart beats. There are a variety of problems that can arise from this particular valve problem, but my son's valve leakage has led to an aneurysm of his upper aorta. This is a potentially deadly problem. It is indeed serious.

My husband and I follow the instruction of our son's physicians, and we are careful and aware of our son's lifestyle. However, we do not subscribe to our cardiologist having the last word; he simply does not. God Himself does. So, in our own way, we respectfully "ignore" negativity, excessive worry, and fretting (over-controlling our son's normal activities, pressure from family members, etc.) We have great hope in our trustworthy God, and we fully expect Him to perform a miracle – or multiple miracles in our son's life. And truth be told, He already has. More than I can count! Every day my son functions as a normal child is a miracle – and there have been some great miracles in addition to the daily ones.

In ending today, I'd like to ask you to re-read verses 36 – 43. Focus on verse 42. Expect to be absolutely overwhelmed when you faithfully trust our trustworthy Lord. May God bless you as we end this week's study. See you next time!

Week Three

Day One

I am so very glad you've decided to join me in another week of study in God's Word. We're going to move back into the Old Testament to the book of Joshua. Please turn to Joshua Chapter 5, and read it in its entirety. Although it isn't a long chapter, it is an important one. Let's look at three points from this chapter, and see if we can make some applications that are relevant to us today. Since these points are each in-depth, I will divide them up over more than one day's study.

Point # 1) In verse 5 we see that the men who had left Egypt in God's mighty deliverance had all been circumcised. We also read that none born during the years in the wilderness had been circumcised. Please write out Joshua 5:5 on the lines below in the translation you have read it from.

_____
_____
_____
_____
_____
_____
_____

When this verse uses the word wilderness, one of its meanings (according to Hebrew Strong's #4057) is "uninhabited land." The point I'd like to make may take some explaining on my part, so please bear with me!

Although many of us were raised in Christian home, a number of us were not. And although those backgrounds may leave us with seemingly nothing in common, we all share one great heritage as Christian homeschoolers; our uninhabited land.

Early in the history of our country, public education was unheard of. People taught their children at home. In fact, a study on the literacy rates in the individual states prior to and following the introduction of mandatory public schooling reveals that Americans were substantially more literate during the former versus the latter. That's a subject you may want to look into on your own, as it is fascinating and holds a unique brand of encouragement to us as Americans who choose to homeschool (see the Recommended Reading List). For our purposes today, however, I simply would like to make note of the fact that home education existed in America prior to the current homeschool movement.

Like the Israelites who left Egypt, our parents did not homeschool, just as their parents did not live out their lives in the Promised Land. There was a gap in time between the man Israel coming to Egypt and the nation of Israel leaving Egypt. Our time gap is that of a previous generation of home education and our current generation of homeschoolers.

We are currently reclaiming our land that has been uninhabited. It truly is hard work building upon a heritage that did not homeschool. We must expect struggle and toil to a certain extent – after all, a foundation can not be laid for future homeschoolers (our children and their children, etc.) if we don't actually work at laying one down.

Today's journaling time is personal, and it may not be a topic you have considered before. I'm going to ask you to write down anything that comes to mind that might be a stumbling block to laying a foundation for the future. And as the context of our reading referred to the parents being circumcised and their children not being circumcised, I would like you to ponder whether there might be any baggage you've carried from your wilderness journey that you need to put down now that you are in a "new land". Ask the Lord to cleanse your heart and gently reveal to you any part of your heritage that needs to be left behind in the wilderness.

Today let's end our time together with prayer.

Father, how I thank you for every woman who longs to be all You have called her to be. And how my heart aches for those who are too afraid to embark upon the journey to their Promised Land with You. May you encourage them all today, Lord, and pour out upon them such love and lavish grace that they will never again be the same. Teach us, Father, so that we will be fit to teach. And build in us and through us a foundation that brings You glory, a firm foundation that our children can stand soundly upon. Thank you Lord. In Jesus' mighty Name we pray – AMEN.

Day Two

Today we are again in Joshua 5, looking at my second point from this chapter. Let's jump right in and read verse 7. Please write down what you believe this verse meant to Joshua. Remember, he was one of the spies that believed they could conquer the land under Moses' leadership, and now he himself is the leader, ready to finally do some conquering.

_____
_____
_____
_____
_____
_____

What might this verse mean to us as Christian's who educate at home?

_____
_____
_____
_____
_____
_____

Point #2) I just love the words, "those who had grown up to take their father's places." Using the KJV and the Hebrew Strong's #6965 for the word "up", we find that this word means "to arise, become powerful; come on the scene, to be established, be confirmed; to be valid; to be proven; to be set, be fixed; to raise up, constitute."

We see from just those portions of the meaning of the word that "raised up" carries quite a lot of weight. And one wonderful day our children will be raised up, established, confirmed, validated, fully ready to leave our homes and walk on into the Promised Land God has for them.

Now please list some goals you hope to achieve in your children's lives.

_____
_____
_____
_____
_____
_____
_____

Ladies, if we could fully and concretely grasp the fact that we are working primarily to equip our children for the next phase of their lives, and that our time with them is limited and finite - how our homes and homeschools would change! Academia is important, but it is not <u>most</u> important! If we equip and prepare our children for every aspect of life, yet leave them unprepared to live the life of God's choosing, then we have failed them. We must choose to work at the most important task first and foremost, and believe that all the other things will be added unto them as well.

Now, look at that list you wrote out on page 29. Does anything on that list seem less important? Is there anything on that list you need to trust God to accomplish while you work to ensure your children know Jesus and His Word intimately? The point of this lesson is not to condemn, for there is no now no condemnation for those that are in Christ. The point is to spur us on to passionately instill a love of Word and a love of Jesus in our children – and to trust Him that the rest will fall into place.

Day Three

Once again we are in Joshua chapter 5, focusing on verse 12 and then on verses 13 – 15.

This is simply my personal opinion, but verse 12 speaks volumes to me about my homeschool journey. Your translation may read differently than mine, so I'll list a few different versions before we discuss the verse further.

NLT – "No manna appeared that day, and it was never seen again. So from that time on the Israelites ate from the crops of Canaan."

KJV – "And the manna ceased on the morrow after they had eaten of the old corn of the land; neither had the children of Israel manna anymore; but they did eat of the fruit of Canaan that year."

HCSB – "And the day after they ate from the produce of the land, the manna ceased. Since there was not more manna for the Israelites, they ate from the crops of the land of Canaan that year."

Point # 3) I am encouraged to know that the Lord will provide me with exactly what I need, in the exact amount I need, only until He knows I no longer have need of it. Then it will cease, and hopefully I won't panic and believe I still need it! He does not change, He is from everlasting to everlasting, and He loves us so. May we realize that even when changes come and His provision seems different than that which we are used to, we can trust Him and know He will take care of us just as He took such great care of the Israelites in Joshua's day.

Have you experienced any areas of change that relate to your homeschool experience? Please write them out and share them if you are in a group setting. If you are doing this study alone, consider sharing these changes and God's subsequent provision (or your fears about the changes) with a friend or fellow homeschooler.

_____
_____
_____
_____
_____
_____
_____
_____

Please read verses 13 –15 one more time. Isn't it good to know that the Lord's angels cannot take sides based on our human performance? That's a thought we just have to expand upon!

God is going to accomplish exactly what He set out to accomplish – and although I am called to obedience as one saved by grace, I cannot mess things up so greatly that Gods' plans are thwarted! It's simply not possible! The heavenly warriors that He commands simply obey Him – they do not fall prey to judgments based on our human strength or frailty.

In other words, our help is sent to aid us even if we stumble around at times on the wrong path. It may take a while longer, we may get knocked around a bit, and we may have tearful regrets, but we cannot undermine God's authority or force our God-sent help in the form of angels to flee from us.

They very same strength available to Joshua is available to us, and we know from Joshua 1:1-9 that it wasn't his own ability or his lack of fear that made him strong. So what are we so afraid of? Spend the time needed prostate before the Lord as Joshua did, and then get up and set about the task He has appointed to you. Be strong and courageous! For His is with you.

Day Four

We will leave the book of Joshua today and move forward to Psalm 15. This is a short Psalm written by David, but it contains some great council to us as Christians living in a fallen world. Take a moment to read all of Psalm 15.

I love the KJV of the last part of verse 4. It reads, "He that sweareth to his own hurt, and changeth not." This verse speaks of keeping our promises even when it hurts. Has it ever been painful for you to keep a commitment you made? Share below.

_____
_____
_____
_____
_____
_____
_____
_____
_____

We have all made commitments and promises that were painful and costly, and while some of them may have been foolish commitments to make, we can certainly learn from them because God wastes nothing.

I believe David desired to share with others some keys to joyful living. And since David loved God so very much, he wanted others to know how to enjoy sweet fellowship with Him as well.

Today my hope is to encourage us first as Christian women, then as homeschool mothers. We are living in an age when the media and our society bombard us with negativity, slander, and evil in every possible format. The only place we might have in our home to escape this bombardment could be in a corner with our Bible! I think David knew a thing or two about feeling surrounded by dark circumstances, some of his own making and others of no fault of his own.

Verse 2 of Psalm 15 encourages us to speak the truth from a sincere heart. I don't know about you, but I cannot do this without the Holy Spirit controlling both my tongue and my heart! God knew this when He placed that verse in His Word. We ought to ask Him to give us hearts that are so sincere that we are only able to speak the truth in love. Let's make that a goal in our prayer life, shall we? Ask Him to grant us that in every relationship we have. In the homeschool sense, we need to bless our children and not speak to them in an unloving manner – not even when we speak the truth.

Is there anyone you wish to share truth with, but aren't sure you can do it in the loving way God desires? Take a moment to write out a brief prayer to the Father, asking Him to work out His will in and through you.

_____
_____
_____
_____
_____
_____
_____
_____
_____
_____

Let's continue in this Psalm, looking at verses 3 and 4. Do we always honor our fellow Christians? Or do we jump at the chance to defame them? What must the Lord think of such a display?

On the same hand, do we compromise or even defend the persistent sinners around us? These may include family or friends, co-workers or peers; or it may simply be the television or movies we choose to observe.

Can we say that we refuse to slander others? If you can, I am so pleased, but the Lord is not finished with me in this area yet! I know that He who began a good work in me will be faithful to complete it.

The final words of Psalm 15 give us encouragement to press on with the Lord to lead a more blameless life. The KJV reads, "He that doeth these things shall never be moved." How greatly I desire to be so cemented in Jesus that I shall never be moved! Praise God, He desires that far more than I do!

Please write out which part of this Psalm you would most like to pass on as a heritage to your children. (Consider writing it out as a prayer)

_____
_____
_____
_____
_____
_____

Now entrust Him to do it! He has promised that His word will not return to Him void. May God bless your day!

Day Five

We'll finish this week's study in the New Testament. Turn with me to Luke chapter 19. Please read the parable of the servants in verses 11 – 27.

Knowing that as believers we have all been entrusted with gifts, how does the reading of these verses impact or convict you?

_____
_____
_____
_____

Does it encourage you to draw out the gifts God has given your children? Specify a gift for each child below. If you are drawing a total blank, ask God to give you a glimpse of His vision for your children.

CHILD	GIFT

Most of what you glean from today's time in the Word will be between you and God, with little commentary from me. There are times when we need to just listen fixedly for what the Lord has to say to us, and I believe this is one of those times. On the lines below, write out any verse (or verses) from our reading in Luke that the Spirit is impressing upon you.

Now please write out how it relates to your life. This does not have to correlate to homeschooling alone; God is deeply interested and involved in every area of your life. Let Him minister to you where you most need it.

Please end today's time by re-reading verse 17 and 26. The implication here is there will be eternal work for us to do based on what we do (or chose not to do) with the talents and work given us in this life. May we run this race in such a way as to get the prize, and use our talents for His glory. Amen to that!

Week Four

Day One

    This week's study time will be spent primarily in a book chock full of wisdom, straight from the mouth of the wisest man ever to walk the face of the earth. Turn with me to Proverbs 29 please. We won't be studying all 27 verses, but let's go ahead and read them. On the lines below write down a verse that seems to just leap off the page at you today.

_____
_____
_____
_____
_____
_____

    I'd like to direct your attention to verse one. I will write it out in the NLT, and then you can write out your translation in order to compare them. "Whoever stubbornly refuses to accept criticism will suddenly be broken beyond repair."

_____
_____
_____
_____
_____
_____

    I wish I could read all the different translations written down! Sometimes I just love to sit and compare the same portion of Scripture in multiple translations; it gives me a more complete grasp of what the Lord is saying through His Word. It can also be a great tool that God uses to drive a point home to me in a clear and specific manner. Your results may be different in studying multiple translations, but I am confident you will be blessed.

    Getting back to our verse! These words penned so long ago by Solomon aptly fit our lives today, whether or not the words themselves seem harsh. Not every reading time will be solely full of encouragement; God also uses His Word to teach and discipline us. Although I dislike ever delivering news that isn't totally positive, I can recognize that there are times when I need to be willing to be God's messenger to facilitate the growth of others.

In this verse Solomon tells us that if we refuse to accept criticism, we will be broken beyond repair. Wow! What a staggering thought! As much as I would like to claim no knowledge of ever having experienced the events described in Proverbs 29:1, I cannot honestly make that claim. I have stubbornly refused criticism and I have been broken beyond repair in certain areas of my life. But the good news is that when the Lord has allowed me to be broken "beyond repair" in any area of my life, it has always been an area He was ready to close the book on! And He has worked in my heart to be more accepting of criticism, as well.

Please write down any reasons you may have for not wanting to accept criticism.

_____
_____
_____
_____
_____
_____

I can think of a wide variety of reasons for disliking criticism, but the reality is that we are all going to give and receive plenty of it, so we ought to learn how to deal with it. And in learning how to accept it we will in turn be better at giving criticism in a God-honoring fashion.

So, how do we learn to deal with the pain and pride involved with being criticized? Well, let's start by asking God to teach us, by His Word and by His Spirit. Will you pray with me?

Father, as homeschooling parents, we are going to be subject to criticism, from inside and outside the church. We need Your help to deal with criticism in a manner that glorifies You. Teach us to see all criticism through Your eyes, and to give criticism with Your voice only. Show us how to love others so deeply that any criticism we might give would only be given for their benefit. And enable us to receive criticism in such a way that we mature due to it. Help us to bring any hurts we receive to You, that You might comfort us. In this way, Lord, let no bitterness take root in our lives. We praise You for Your continuing work in each of our hearts and homes. In Your Name we pray, AMEN.

Day Two

We will remain in the 29th chapter of Proverbs for today's lesson. Verse 25 will be our starting point. It reads, "Fearing people is a dangerous trap, but to trust the Lord means safety." (NLT)

As homeschool moms, we might regularly think of both "fear" and "safety". We may have fear about what others might say or do if our children are out in public or playing out of doors during the school day. We may feel more in control of our children and their safety if we monitor and regulate their every movement. But, this verse teaches us that we lay a dangerous trap for ourselves when we fear people. We learn here the only real place of safety lies in totally trusting the Lord.

When we encounter times of fear in our lives, we can say aloud, "To trust the Lord means safety!" Let's take that to the bank spiritually. I'll tell you what, if Solomon the wise said that fearing people is a dangerous trap, then I don't want to be fearful!

So when those times of fear, anxiety, and worry come up on you, simply refuse to fall in to that trap of emotion. Instead, speak God's Word aloud and ask Him to give you wisdom and discernment. If there is grave danger about, the Lord is more than able to make you aware of it. But fearful living is absolutely not God's plan for you. He tells us to fear not 365 times in His Word. That tells me that there isn't a day of the year that I can justify fear over trust in Jesus Christ.

Now it's your turn. Please read over Proverbs 29:20 and take some time to think and pray about the verse. Allow God's Spirit to reveal to You what He would have you to learn from it. Write out your insights on the lines below. I've placed some prompts for you to use – but if you don't need them, don't use them!

How does this verse apply to you as a wife?

_____
_____
_____
_____

As a mother?

_____
_____
_____
_____

As a Christian involved in a local church?

_____
_____
_____
_____

As you train up your children?

_____
_____
_____
_____

In regard to people who disagree with homeschooling?

_____
_____
_____
_____

I think this is a good place to end today's study. Be encouraged, ladies, you are staying the course and staying in the Word! God will faithfully complete the good work He began in you.

Day Three

Let's focus on two verses today that deal with our emotions. Proverbs 29:5 and 11 will be our references for this lesson. Once again I will list the New Living Translation so that you can read the verses the way I'm reading them.

Proverbs 29:5 – "To flatter people is to lay a trap for their feet." And verse 11 – "A fool gives full vent to anger, but a wise person quietly holds it back."

Do you struggle with either of these emotions? I know I certainly do! Flattery comes easily to people-pleasers, although we may not give flattery falsely or with ill-intent. It simply is very natural for us to compliment others. Anger is also an emotion all humans must deal with. Even if you are not an angry person, chances are there is someone in your life that is.

Think of a time when you were flattered by or flattered another. Write about it on the lines below.

_____
_____
_____
_____
_____
_____
_____
_____
_____

Now do the same with a time when you were angry, or when another person was angry with you.

_____
_____
_____
_____
_____
_____
_____
_____
_____

Do these thoughts bring back positive memories and emotions, or negative ones? Dear ladies, I am not trying to cause you pain or to re-open old wounds. I would like us to see from these verses that by applying God's Word to our hearts and lives we can live in such a way that our emotions are Spirit-controlled, and not under the control of the flesh.

This relates to homeschooling in one primary area in my mind; my witness to my children. I am not called to let loose a volley of anger, not toward any one at any time. Does that mean a Christian woman should never be angry? Well, no. That isn't possible, and God doesn't ask us to do what cannot be done. Rather, we are to deal frankly and openly with our feelings in a prompt manner, so that there is no emotional build-up lying just beneath the surface.

You see, ladies, we can stuff and stuff so much emotion that it literally rots away inside of us, and then one day one last thing tips the scales and – KABOOM – we find ourselves giving full vent to our anger in a very foolish manner. I'd like to discuss the portion of verse 11 which says that a wise person quietly holds back their anger. How can that be done? By giving control of the situation to the Lord, and by being honest with Him. Only He can take our brutal honesty. The rest of the world probably cannot! If further words need to be spoken regarding an issue, the Lord is able to arrange a time where God-honoring words can be spoken. That is what it means to me to "quietly hold back" my anger.

Please look up the word anger in you Bible's dictionary, index, or concordance. List a few verses below that address anger. If you don't have any reference tools in your Bible, I've listed some verses that you can look up.

_____
_____
_____
_____
_____
_____
_____

(My verses are Proverbs 15:1, Ephesians 4:26, James 1:20, Exodus 34:6, 2 Samuel 12:5, Nehemiah 9:17, Psalm 30:5, and Psalm 78:38)

Verse 5 of Proverbs 29 speaks of flattery. It says that flattering people is like laying a trap for their feet. What do you think that means? In what way is flattery a trap?

___

Now please read Psalm 5:9, and write down what it says about flattery.

_____
_____
_____

_____
_____
_____

Psalm 5 seems to imply that flattery is not truthful, and that those that flatter others are really seeking their own good will. That being said, could there be a difference between flattering someone and complimenting them? Let's use Noah Webster's 1828 Dictionary to find out.

>Flatter: 1. To soothe by praise; to gratify self-love by praise or obsequiousness. (Mr. Webster references Proverbs 29 in this edition of his dictionary)
>   2. To please, to gratify as to flatter one's vanity or pride.
>   3. To praise falsely.
>   4. To raise false hopes by representations not well founded.
>   5. To wheedle; to coax

Flattery: False praise; commendation bestowed for the purpose of gaining favor and influence, or to accomplish some purpose.

>Compliment: 2. To congratulate
>   3. To bestow a present; to manifest kindness or regard for, by present or other favor.

So, there is a certain discriminatory difference between these two words, but the difference can be summed up as the intent of the heart. Let us be so driven by God and His Word that we know the intent of our heart before the words ever reach our lips. This is a noble goal for a homeschooling mother, since we have little students learning from all that we do. Let's continue to lay a solid foundation for each of our homeschooled children to build upon.

Day Four

For our fourth day of study this week, we are going to be looking at two different parts of the Word of God. Let's begin this lesson with prayer. Please join me.

Loving Father, faithful Lord, today I ask that You would be with us as we study Your Word. May this brief lesson touch our hearts and draw us ever closer to You. Let the women who complete this lesson today be filled with Your joy and empowered anew to fulfill all the plans and purposes You have for them. We praise You for choosing us to take part in this ministry of homeschooling, and we thank You that You hear our prayers. In Your Holy Name we pray, AMEN.

The words that are inside of me today feel so much bigger than I am able to express. I fear that my words will not convey all that is inside my heart – possibly something like the way our English words fail to fully express the Hebrew language with its beautiful complexity. By the grace of God, some small portion of my heart's desire will come through onto the pages today.

Psalm 18 is a fairly long Psalm, so you do not have to read all of it right now, but it is listed in the rear of your book as today's selected reading. David is conveying a lot to us in this Psalm – and I am sure there was a lot more that could have been said! After all, he had been rescued from King Saul, among many other enemies. Today's focus is on being rescued, and on how we can help to "rescue" others, even during our most trying times in life.

Here are today's verses; please read them all. I have listed them in the NLT at the end of today's lesson, just in case you would like to read them in the translation I am writing out of. Please begin with Psalm 18:19 and continue reading verses 28-36, 39, 46, 48, and 49.

Please record which of those verses strikes you most today.

_____
_____
_____
_____
_____
_____

Today I think that verse 32 is most comforting to me personally. It reads, "God arms me with strength; He has made my way safe." (NLT) Since we know that God has carefully written all the days of each of our individual lives in His book, it is good to know that He has made the ways safe for each of us as we live out those days. If God were not present with David, could He have made David's way safe? No – a far-off God could not accomplish such a thing. Our God is not far-off; He is near to us, making our way safe each and every day.

Now, I'd like to move to Job 4 in the Bible. Here one of Job's "friends" is speaking, and since we only want to look at a portion of Scripture here, let's read verses 3 – 7. Please write out which of these verses stands out to you most today.

___

Let's look at verse 4. I love the implication here that our words can strengthen and steady others. As a homeschooling mother, I need to know that my words are able to do such things! I don't just wish for it, I need to know it! I don't want to lose that understanding when difficulties enter my life. During my greatest struggles in life I still want to serve the Lord by strengthening and steadying others. That is a lofty goal, I know, but my God is able to accomplish it through His Spirit within me. He wants to do it through each one of us – starting at home with our children and husbands and spreading out from there.

Let's move forward to Psalm 18 once again. I would like you to write out the benefits or blessings mentioned in the verses listed below. List anything that strikes you – God's blessing come in a variety of ways!

Verse 19
___

Verse 28
___

Verse 29
___

Verse 30
___

Verse 31

Verse 32

Verse 33

Verse 34

Verse 35

Verse 36

Verse 39

Verse 46

Verse 48

Verse 49

    I want us to see all that the Lord does in the course of rescuing us. He loves us so dearly that not only does He rescue us, He leads us to a place of safety; He delights in us; He brings light to our life; He lights up our darkness; He strengthens us to scale the walls in our path; His way is perfect; His promises prove true; He is a shield; He makes our way safe; He makes us surefooted; He leads us safely along our mountain heights; He prepares and strengthens us for our tasks and our battles; He shields us with His salvation; His right hand supports each one of us; His gentleness makes each of us great; He has made a wide path for our feet, that we might not slip; He has armed us with strength; He lives! And He is exalted! He holds us safely beyond the reach of our enemies; He will be praised among the nations.

Today's lesson is longer than usual, but I deeply desire for each of us to see clearly how much God cares for us! He loves us like crazy! How would our lives change if we really got a hold of that?!

Comparing that compilation of blessings and benefits to our reading of Job 4, I ask the question: How do we keep from losing our ability to encourage and support others? Shouldn't our "reverence for God" give us "confidence?" (See Job 4:6 NLT) It surely should. The above list of things that God has done and will do for me enables me to continue to bless and encourage others, even when life ought to get me down, provided I actually <u>believe</u> that God applies all those benefits to my life, not just to David's life.

Friends, in closing I just want you to know that God does speak those blessings over your lives. He believes in you so much! Now you just go on and believe in yourself. God bless you all.

New Living Translation Verses

Verse 19: "He led me to a place of safety; he rescued me because he delights in me."

28: "LORD, you have brought light to my life; my God, you light up my darkness."

29: "In your strength I can crush an army; with my God I can scale any wall."

30: "As for God, his way is perfect. All the LORD's promises prove true. He is a shield to all who look to him for protection."

31: "For who is God except the LORD? Who but our God is a solid rock?"

32: "God arms me with strength; he has made my way safe."

33: "He makes me as surefooted as a deer, leading me safely along the mountain heights."

34: "He prepares me for battle; he strengthens me to draw a bow of bronze."

35: "You have given me the shield of your salvation. Your right hand supports me; your gentleness has made me great."

36: "You have made a wide path for my feet to keep them from slipping."

39: "You have armed me with strength for the battle; you have subdued my enemies under my feet."

46: "The LORD lives! Blessed be my rock! May the God of my salvation be exalted!"

48: "and rescues me from my enemies. You hold me safe beyond the reach of my enemies; you save me from violent opponents."

49: "For this, O LORD, I will praise you among the nations; I will sing joyfully to your name."

Day Five

Today's lesson contains some difficult reading. It focuses on a great time of trial during the days of King David. Trials caused in part by his own son, Absalom. Please turn to 2 Samuel and skim over chapters 15 and 16, stopping to focus on verses 5 – 14 of the sixteenth chapter. Your daily reading guide in the rear of your study listed 2 Samuel 15 as the portion of Scripture assigned to Day Three of this week's study, so hopefully the chapter is still somewhat fresh in your mind.

In these 2 brief chapters I find a fascinating cast of characters. I truly do not understand how anyone could ever claim that the Bible is boring! Television in our current era is brimming with "reality TV." programs – people are nearly obsessed with them! I personally believe, however, that there may be more for me to chew on in this handful of verses than there is in all those television programs combined. And this is only one portion of the Bible! We ought to turn off the television (or the square-idol as we refer to it in my home) and crack open the Living Word!

Let's review those involved in our look at the Word today.
Who was David?

_____
_____

Who was Absalom?

_____
_____

Who went with David as he fled Jerusalem? (hint: see verse 15, 18)

_____

Who were Absalom's advisors? (verse 34, 37)

_____
_____

Who was Ziba? (Chapter 16:1-4)

_____
_____

Who was Shimei?

_____
_____

In the course of this day, King David experienced treachery and betrayal at the hands of his own son, discovered which of his followers were faithful to him (and which were not), prayed against his former advisor Ahithophel, wept as he climbed the Mount of Olives, left his capital city with disgrace and mourning, and was cursed and assaulted by an angry relative of the late King Saul. All this in one day!

I have had many homeschool days that were far from perfect, but I have never had a day that compares to this particular day in the life of King David. While my personal feeling is that David would have been wise to seek out God's direction prior to fleeing Jerusalem (rather than reacting to the bad news of Absalom's takeover in fear), I also know that I can learn so much from his reaction to the assault by Shimei son of Gera.

Please re-read verses 5-8 of 2 Samuel chapter 16. Shimei's accusations against King David are inaccurate. Can you explain in what way?

_____
_____
_____
_____
_____
_____

Not only was David innocent in regard to Saul's death, he was in fact never willing to kill Saul, even though it may have seemed justified. Although David was guilty of having Urriah the Hittite murdered (see 2 Samuel 11), he repented and accepted God's chastisement (see 2 Samuel 12). I am quite certain from reading the Psalms (Psalm 51 in particular), that God does not give us a taste of our own medicine, but rather He lavishes us with His grace. Even though David could reason that Shimei's words were unfounded and untrue, how do you think he felt as he walked along with stones and curses falling upon him?

_____
_____
_____
_____
_____
_____

Now, here is the link between this scene and our lives as we homeschool our children. We are each going to have trying days. We will each likely receive "curses and stoning" from others, in a vast array of forms (harsh accusations, insensitive words, unfair generalizations, etc.), and we need to know where we stand with the Lord beforehand. Verse 12 tells us that David understood that the Lord is able to avenge any unjust wrongs committed against His children. It is wise counsel for us to speak no unnecessary evil in the face of harsh criticism, and to rest in the knowledge that God can bless us as we trust Him in our trials. There's one more person I'd like to look at from this story. Please glance quickly at 2 Samuel 13. Who is guilty of the heinous crime committed against Tamar?

_____

Do we see any evidence that King David dealt with Absalom's grave sin?
_____
_____

No, it appears that he did not. One of David's few great failures came in the area of disciplining his children. Although I cannot possibly know the reasons for David's neglect in this aspect of his parenting, I suspect that this problem did not begin with his children, but with the many mothers of his children. Ladies, if we fail to discipline our children, they will suffer. I can attest to that from my own childhood experiences. And if we fail to deal with our own parasitic sins, our children may not be equipped to deal with those same sins in their own lives. My evidence in support of this claim? 2 Samuel 16:21-23. What David had done in secret, Absalom did in the full light of day for all to see. When our children grow up seeing particular sins repeated over and over again, they can very easily take those sins to an even more brazen level and think nothing of it.
Praise God, this is not always the case! He is able to deliver children from generational sin in His great mercy before it taints their lives, but I don't want to desensitize my children to any sin! Ladies, may we desire to leave a heritage of godliness and nothing less than that! I'll see you next week.

Week Five

Day One

Last week we looked into one brief segment of David's life. We saw that any sin we cling to can in turn cling to our children. Today let's look at the opposite end of the spectrum - leaving our children a godly heritage. Please read Isaiah 38:19. Write your translation on the lines below.

_____
_____
_____
_____
_____
_____

The NLT reads, "Only the living can praise you as I do today. Each generation can make known your faithfulness to the next."

Upon reading this verse, I am struck twofold. First, I see that I am to impart to my children <u>all</u> of God's mighty deeds (those listed in the Bible), and I am also to tell my children <u>all</u> of the things God has done in my own life. The way I can relate the first sentence of this verse to the second sentence is to speak of God's faithfulness in my life and in His testimony to me through the Bible at every opportunity I have while I am on this earth. Those who are dead – spiritually or physically – are not able to praise Him. It is the honor of the people who belong to Him to praise Him. Please write down at least one praise you have for each member of your immediate family.

<u>Family Member</u>	<u>Praise to God</u>

Let's try to make this a regular par of our day-to-day lives.

If we would speak blessings over our children and spouses, and would greatly praise our Father for the treasures He gives us, we would see transformation happen in our homes. And we would impact the next generation in a way that could well impact the rest of the world. I don't think we can comprehend what God would do with a people that never ceased to praise Him.

Let's look up a few verses that teach us about praising our God. Please write the verses out as follows:

Psalm 9:1 -

Praise is sincere, from the heart. It speaks aloud of what God has done.

2 Chronicles 5:13, 14 -

True praise causes us to cease from all internal and external activity as we are fixated on the Lord.

Psalm 103:1, 2 -

Encourage yourself to praise Him; do not hesitate to recall to mind all He has done and will continue to do.

Acts 2:25, 26 -

Our praise affects our circumstances. It also affects our hearts in the midst of our circumstances.

Here we have briefly touched on praise, and already we see great evidence that part of a godly heritage is an attitude of praise. Raising our children in a home environment focused on praising God and recounting His mighty deeds, we can prepare the next generation to live a life of praise-filled blessing.

Day Two

Today we're going to look at Matthew 18:1-6. Please read the verses now.

What did Jesus say would happen to anyone causing a "little one" to lose faith?

_____
_____
_____
_____

We see in verses 2-4 that Jesus deeply cares about children. They truly are precious in His sight. In verse 6, the phrase "little one" can mean not only a child, but any young believer. Our duty here is to children in all aspects; literal children of a young age, and spiritual children in Christ, regardless of age.

Verse 3 tells us to turn from our sins and become as little children. Obviously, we cannot physically become children again. When you promise to do something for a very young child, do they doubt you or fully trust in you? They completely believe in the adults surrounding them! An influential adult in the life of a child is a powerful force – what the adult says is absolute truth to the young child.

Jesus wants us to trust in Him with that same kind of absolute assurance. This kind of believing leaves virtually no room for doubt. The humility He speaks of in verse four cannot be found in people that grumble and complain their way through life. We must cease our questioning of the Lord and choose to accept His authority in our lives.

Let's look at verse six again. How do you feel when you encounter someone who attempts to cast doubt on your belief?

_____
_____
_____
_____

How do you think others are impacted when you cast doubt upon their belief?

_____
_____
_____
_____

Do we truly accept the fact that the Lord has a unique call upon every believer's life? Of course we are all going to answer "yes" to that question, so I'll ask another. Do we truly accept the fact that we have no God-given right to tell others what their calling is and is not? It's a bit more difficult to answer that question with an honest "yes".

Please read Paul's words in 1 Corinthians 12:14-17, and then read verses 21-26. Please write out the words of verse 21.

_____
_____
_____
_____

The NLT reads, "The eye can never say to the hand, 'I don't need you.' The head can't say to the feet, 'I don't need you.'"

How often do we adopt an "I-don't-need-you" attitude? The apostle Paul tells us in verse 26 that if one suffers, we all suffer. If we truly took this verse to heart, we might be more willing to "clean up our act", so to speak, in order to stop undue church sufferings.

So what does all of this have to do with homeschooling, you ask? We are regularly criticized as a group at large. Sometimes by our fellow Christians. We know how painful it is to be misunderstood when answering God's call. I'd like to place a challenge before the homeschool community, including myself.

Let's stop bashing other Christians! Permanently!

There are distinct differences between Christians who homeschool and Christians who do not homeschool. Often times, both sides feel that they are 100% correct. I can tell you exactly how I feel about the issue; the problem with that is that my feelings are subjective. I must align my personal feelings with God's Word, and walk out in faith my personal call from God.

Let's look at some Scriptures that can help us keep our hearts pure before God. After reading each verse please write down any insights you have regarding judging fellow believers and the reliability of our feelings and emotions.

I Corinthians 12:18 – "But God made our bodies with many parts, and He has put each part just where He wants it."

_____
_____
_____

Galatians 5:26 – "Let us not become conceited, or irritate one another, or be jealous of one another."

_____
_____
_____
_____

Psalm 51:10 – "Create in me a clean heart, O God. Renew a right spirit within me."

_____
_____
_____
_____

Proverbs 24:12b – "For God knows all hearts, and He sees you."

_____
_____
_____
_____

Proverbs 27:19 – "As a face is reflected in water, so the heart reflects the person."

_____
_____
_____
_____

Jeremiah 17:9 – "The human heart is most deceitful and desperately wicked. Who really knows how bad it is?"

_____
_____
_____
_____

Psalm 103:13, 14 – "The Lord is like a father to His children; tender and compassionate to those who fear Him. For He understands how weak we are; He knows we are only dust."

I believe we can safely say that God alone knows the heart of man. Jeremiah teaches me that I cannot even know my own heart! If I rely on my feelings and emotions, I will be deceived.

So what are we to do when we come up against unfair criticism? What do we say when we believe we know what is best for another person? Perhaps we should do absolutely nothing! Pray, pray, and pray again! The only assurance we have of acting or reacting as God would have is by seeking Him before we act or react! This does not mean we are to suffer abuse or ignore blatant sin. It simply means we ought to trust God enough to allow Him to tell us what we ought to do or not do.

Just imagine the positive impact this kind of living could have on our marriages, churches, and communities. Imagine how much more prepared our children would be to live out their faith in love if we were to impart this type of living to them. Just imagine how God-honoring that would be!

Day Three

Part of being a Christian involves interacting with other Christians. While we expect our dealings with non-believers to be strained at times, we don't always like to admit that tensions arise among believers. The Lord knew full well that our sin nature and the enemy's tactics would affect our lives inside and outside the church building's walls. He graciously provides us with the wisdom we need in His Word. Let's read 1 Corinthians 12:12-31.

Verse 18 tells us that we have each been placed exactly where He wants us. Is that always pleasant? Or are there times when we wish He would place us somewhere else? Sometimes being smack dab in the middle of our calling is the last place we want to be. Have you ever tried to run away from God's call on your life? If so, please give a brief description.

_____
_____
_____
_____
_____
_____
_____

I know I have certainly tried to pull a Jonah at times! I have also attempted to convince God to see things my way. But you know what? I can look back now and see that I could not become whom God was making me if I did not go where He led me. And the same holds true today. While it may not be any easier for me to remain in the midst of a trying ministry, it has gotten easier to follow the Lord in my ministry. Let's just say I'm not so tempted to run to Tarshish instead of Ninevah anymore!

What does verse 22 say about the parts of the body that seem most weak?

_____
_____

Do you ever feel weak? Or perhaps you look at others in the body and pass judgment upon them. Maybe you compare yourself to other believers and feel you just don't measure up. Verses 23-24 teach us that the "less-honorable" parts of the body are treated with the most care. Can you think of any examples of this in your own life?

_____
_____

Please read verse 26 again. If a believer leaves the body because he or she feels "less honorable", are we all affected? Yes! We all suffer, according to God's Word. And when one of us is honored or is rejoicing? We are all glad. If you feel "less honorable", or if you view another person in that light, please realize that it is not so. God has intertwined us all, that we might glorify Him.

Now, to relate this to homeschooling, do you have a child that learns differently than your other children? Or maybe you don't feel like you fit in at church, if you are the only homeschooler? Perhaps your extended family loves the Lord but doesn't agree with your decision to homeschool. God knows how hard it is to feel "different", to feel "less honorable" than other believers. He also knows that it hurts more to feel set apart within the body than it does to be different from the world at large. He cares so very much about every aspect of your life, dear one, and He wants you to turn to Him and allow Him to comfort you. He also wants you to learn what verse 31 tells us, "And in any event, you should desire the most helpful gifts." (NLT) So, in any situation, my goal should be to desire the most helpful gifts. Not the attention-grabbing gifts, but the most helpful ones. Could I draw just one more parallel? Raising our children to be the church of the future, homeschooling them through thick and thin, hanging on for dear life and believing that God will finish what He started – contributing to a generation that will change the world for Jesus – ladies, that is the most helpful gift you can ever give. Press on today and tomorrow and all the tomorrows to come. It is <u>so</u> worth it!

Day Four

We're nearing the end of our fifth week of study. I hope this short journey through God's Word has been as meaningful to you as it has been to me. This lesson will mainly focus on one of the primary tools God uses to teach us and to reach others. Let's look at 1 Corinthians 13 together, and learn some more about love.

We're going to be reading the entire chapter during today's study, but first I'd like to look at verse 2. Please write out this verse in your own words on the lines below.

_____
_____
_____
_____

I am reading this verse in both the New Living Translation and the King James Version, keeping my Strong's Concordance close at hand. I really want us to get a grasp of what our primary goal ought to be as we home educate our children. It's pretty simple to say, "We need to be loving people; we need to teach our kid's to love." But what isn't simple is making that a reality. Since it isn't an easy task to accomplish, we know we must have God's help in the matter. Please read the portion of verse 2 below, in both the NLT and the KJV.

"…and knew everything about everything, but didn't love others, what good would I be?" (NLT)

"…and all knowledge, and though I have all faith, so that I could remove mountains, and have not charity, I am nothing." (KJV)

The NLT poses the question, "What good would I be?" The KJV seems to answer, "I am nothing." As much as I want my children to be knowledgeable once they leave home, I would not be pleased if they amounted to "nothing" spiritually. Yet these verses are telling us that is what they will be if they fail to have love! So how do we make sure they have love, or charity? Let's see if the rest of the chapter 13 can help us out any. Please read all 13 verses of the chapter now.

Verse 8 tells us that knowledge will vanish, and verse 9 says that all our knowledge is only partial knowledge. Think of that, fellow homeschool mothers! All your efforts to teach your children will at best result in only partial knowledge! Ouch!! But the good news is found in verses 12 and 13. How does verse 12 describe our ability to see?

_____
_____

One day we will no longer see through darkened glass. But for now, we can only impart partial knowledge to our children because we are only able to know in part! The NLT says "All that I know now is partial and incomplete, but then I will know everything completely, just as God knows me now." (verse 12b) Knowing that our teaching will be incomplete at best doesn't give us cause to cease homeschooling or to become lax in our teaching; rather, it allows us to run our race with perseverance. (see Hebrews 12:1-2)

The most uplifting part of our study today is found in the last verse of Chapter 13. Three things will endure from this life on into eternity. What are those three things?

_____

_____

Which of those things is the greatest?

_____

Love. Our faith will endure, our hope will endure, and above all love will endure. Do you teach with love? Oh, then it will surely remain throughout eternity! Does it require your faith to work at this task of homeschooling? Do you have hope in the Lord with regard to your children and their future? Then it will tarry in eternity! Yet that which we do in love will be measured beyond all else.

Verse 13 in the King James Version uses the word "abideth". It is listed in Strong's Exhaustive Concordance, Greek #3306, as the word meno (pronounce men-oh). It means "to remain, to sojourn, not to depart, to continue to be present; to continue to be, not to perish, to last, endure; to wait for, await one." Can I draw a conclusion that might seem a bit larger than life? I am encouraged as this verse seems to imply that what I do in this life (in faith, hope, and love), will not depart from me now, will continue to be present, and will wait for me in eternity.

Ladies, what we do in love spans the reaches of all time. It hangs on with us in the here and now, and it awaits us on the other side of this life. How can that be? It is a mystery that only God can fully explain. However, we know it to be true since it is recorded in God's Word. Keep on in love, and know it awaits you in heaven.

Day Five

We're going to end this week in the Old Testament learning from the life of the prophet Elisha and his servant Gehazi. In 2 Kings chapter 2 we read that Elisha refused to leave Elijah, even though Elijah's earthly ministry was drawing to a close. Elisha's earthly ministry had not yet been fully completed. He stayed near Elijah and had faith that the Lord would enable him to carry on as Elijah's successor.

In verses 19-22 we see the beginning of Elisha's ministry to the people of Israel. But then we find an interesting passage of Scripture in verses 23-25. Please read them and then write out a synopsis of what transpired.

_____
_____
_____
_____
_____
_____
_____
_____

My children have a wonderful series of Bible videos that are very accurate, yet the movie that tells the story of Elijah's departure and Elisha's time as a prophet doesn't mention this incident! Is it any wonder? I doubt that a re-telling of these verses would be enjoyable to many children! Yet I can't help but wonder - would our children be more cautious with their words if they knew of this tale?

What can we learn here? All of God's Word is able to teach us, so there is something here that can aid us in our walk with the Lord. But what? What do you learn from this grisly tale? (pun intended!)

_____
_____
_____
_____
_____
_____
_____

How I wish I could read your response! I cannot imagine my children suffering such a gruesome fate, but I do want them to understand that their attitudes and words can be deadly. One thing I have learned from verses 23-24 is that I am to treat my spiritual leaders with respect. I also see that Elisha continued with his ministry immediately after the deaths of these forty-two boys. From this portion of Scripture I can learn to walk in my ministry and leave my emotions with the Lord – He is obviously able to handle my enemies; all the consequences of my trust in Him will lie at His feet.

Now I'd like to skip ahead in this book. Quickly skim over 2 Kings 4:8-36, focusing on verses 31 and 34-35. What kind of faith did Elisha have?

___

Contrast Elisha's faith to that of his servant Gehazi. How was Gehazi's "faith" different?

___

I don't know about you, but I never want to be the type of student that fails to learn the most important lessons from my teacher! I believe Gehazi had a genuine interest in the work of the Lord, at least in some measure. But somewhere along the way he began to trade faith for doubt, and contentment for longing. As we move on to Chapter 5 of 2 Kings, we see Gehazi's ultimate demise. Please read 2 Kings 5:9-27.

What was Naaman's initial reaction?

___

Do we ever react in a like manner when the Lord requires something of us? Human tendency is to shy away from menial tasks; there is a part of us that wants to be in the spotlight. At times we share Naaman's reaction when God asks us to do something. Maybe some of us reacted this way when God began to call us to homeschool our children. Briefly write down your initial reaction to God's call on your life.

___

Thankfully, the Lord is patient. He draws us to Him in increments at times, wooing us and changing our hearts. Naaman was persuaded by his officers, and the Lord healed him of his leprosy.

Did Elisha accept Naaman's gifts?_____Instead, he deferred the glory to God and sent Naaman home in peace. Naaman had peace, Elisha had contentment, but Gehazi had greed. He resorted to lie after lie, which only fueled his greed. But the prophet of the Lord knew Gehazi's heart, just as the Lord Himself knows our hearts. So Gehazi left Elisha's presence and went away with Naaman's illness.

Ladies, when we choose to leave our peace and our contentment in exchange for our greed, we inherit the ills of the world. Our longings can seem justified or legitimate (more curriculum, a newer vehicle, a larger house for our growing family, etc.) but when we turn our focus from God to our wants and desires, we abandon our hope of receiving those things from the Father. We may be able to find a way to get what we want, but we will surely make some type of trade in the process. May we find only growing peace and contentment as we fulfill our call to homeschool, and trust Him to meet our needs as He sees fit one day at a time.

Week Six

Day One

This week we will begin in the Old Testament book of Ecclesiastes. Solomon wrote this book a few thousand years ago, but its lessons are applicable today. Please turn to Ecclesiastes chapter ten.

Verse one of the tenth chapter reads this way in the New Living Translation, "Dead flies will cause even a bottle of perfume to stink! Yes, an ounce of foolishness can outweigh a pound of wisdom and honor." Please write this verse on the lines below from the translation you are reading, so that you are able to compare both versions.

_____
_____
_____
_____

Now please read verse 11 of the same chapter of Ecclesiastes. I will again show you the NLT version of this verse and you can write it out in your translation on the lines below.

"It does no good to charm a snake after it has bitten you." (NLT)

Your translation:

_____
_____

Wisdom and folly. Snake charming. Homeschool. Hmm… do you think we can draw any conclusions about our homeschooling from these verses?

I can't speak for you, but I know I don't want to smell like dead flies! Only with the Lord's grace and mercy in my life am I able to not "stink it up"! Sometimes I think I'm all dolled up and smelling pretty, but in reality I smell like dead bugs. At other times I smell lovely, a fragrant incense to the Lord. The difference? John 15 living – when I let His love flow through me, I bring Him glory.

Solomon teaches us in verse one that an ounce of foolishness can totally undo the effects of a pound of wisdom and honor. Wisdom can take a lifetime to acquire; honor only comes to us after it has been earned time and again. And a tiny amount of foolishness can strip them both away.

So in our homes, in our churches, in our relationships, may we find ourselves leaning more and more upon Jesus, the One who gives true wisdom and who deserves all honor. If we could just abide in Him continually, and love the way He has called us to love, then we would have families and churches bearing more fruit than we could dream of!

Do you have an area of your life that could use some fruit? Is there a portion of your homeschool day that seems a bit barren? Write out a prayer to God, yielding to Him, and invite Him to live out His great love through you in that situation. Pray believing; our God is able!

_____
_____
_____
_____
_____
_____
_____
_____
_____

Now let's move on to verse 11. I'll write this verse out in the NIV, NLT and KJV.

"If a snake bites before it is charmed, there is no profit for the charmer." (NIV)

"It does no good to charm a snake after it has bitten you." (NLT)

"Surely the serpent will bite without enchantment; and the babbler is no better." (KJV)

Each of these three translations of Ecclesiastes 10:11 provides us with a unique lesson as Christian homeschoolers. Let's look at the King James Version first. This verse equates a "babbler" with an untamed serpent. The word babbler means just that; one who babbles, speaks, or talks. (See Strong's Hebrew #3956) So, anyone who speaks is capable of being as harmful as a snake that is not tamed! Our speech affects all areas of life; let us use our mouths to edify others, and guard against having a "forked-tongue".

Next, let's look at the New International Version of verse 11. If our children move into the world without the ability to control their tongues, they will be much like the snake that bites before it is charmed. The snake charmer must work diligently at taming the snake, in the hope of turning a profit one day. Likewise, we work diligently at training our children, in the hope of one day profiting our society. But if our children are "untamed", there may be no such profit.

Lastly, let's examine Ecclesiastes 10:11 from the New Living Translation. Please read that verse again. Have you ever felt the sting of something that you didn't really expect? I mean, has it ever hurt you terribly when something went awry after you had invested much of yourself? All wounds hurt, but this kind of pain can be uniquely excruciating. Why? Because the hurt runs deeper in direct relation to the amount of ourselves poured into something.

I relate this to our homeschool journey in this way; guard your heart! We are called to love everyone, but Jesus does not ask us to give all of ourselves to everyone in our lives. Give only what He asks you to give. Don't pour all of your heart into every relationship! Some people may not be able to handle all of our passion, and the results can be painful for each person involved.

Listen carefully. I am in no way telling you to withdraw from and neglect relationships. I am simply reiterating what Jesus said in Matthew 7:6, "Don't give what is holy to unholy people. Don't give pearls to swine! They will trample the pearls, then turn and attack you." (NLT)

Let me try to make this more clear. Ecclesiastes 10 and Matthew 7 do not promote judgment or hatred on the part of Christ's followers. But they do tell us that we don't have to give all of ourselves to everyone in our lives, believers or unbelievers. Let's face facts, if we lived our lives giving 100% of all we are to everyone around us, we'd be exhausted and they would be too!

Can you think of a time in your homeschooling journey when you were exhausted because you gave 100% of yourself and your passion to something or someone? Please share on the lines below.

_____
_____
_____
_____
_____
_____
_____
_____
_____

Please read all of Ecclesiastes 10 and Matthew 7 today to get a more complete picture of God's Word. When we dig into God's Word regularly, we are more fully able to understand how He desires for us to live.

Day Two

I'd like to open today's lesson time with prayer.

Father, we have nearly finished this brief look into Your Word, and we know You have so much more to teach us. May we commit to You this day the desires of our hearts, that You might live through us in Your love, that we could in turn pour out Your love on our children. May all our efforts to raise up our children in the way they should go bring glory to You, O Lord. In Jesus' Name we pray, AMEN.

Turn in your Bible to Matthew 1:17. What does this short verse summarize?

_____
_____
_____
_____

The first 16 verses of Matthew 1 speak of Jesus' genealogy. While this may not mean much to us as Gentile believers, it meant quite a lot to the Israelite people. Since the book of Matthew was written primarily for the Jews, we can learn much from the book by thinking in Jewish terms.

Please read Genesis 17:7, and write out what it states.

_____
_____
_____
_____

Now please copy the words of Psalm 78:6 on these lines, after reading verses 4-8.

_____
_____
_____
_____

While our translations may vary a bit, they all imply the importance of passing a heritage to the next generation. Jewish people have many beautiful customs. While observing customs does not make us right with God, we as Christians could learn much from Jews attitude toward the Lord. It is in fact so interesting that you may wish to study it in your family's homeschool.

But what does this have to do with Christians who homeschool in this modern age? Well, if our unchanging God cared so much about the heritage passed on to the previous generations of His children, we can be certain He also cares about the godly heritage our children will receive.

We have talked about leaving a heritage to our children previously in this study. It is a subject very dear to my heart. I want so much for the children in my sphere of influence to know and understand God's Word, I think I would do just about anything to facilitate it. Oh, that our children would be a generation that knows and loves the Word, that speaks and prays God's Word in power and that ignites a fire that the world cannot put out! So how do we accomplish a task of that magnitude?

While it most certainly will not be easy, it is achievable. First and foremost, our father's need to take time to impart God's Word to our children. Why the fathers? Don't mothers typically do most of the teaching in a family homeschool? Personally, I believe God richly blesses spiritual leadership of the men in our families. Since they are called to the position of spiritual leadership by God, they most certainly should step up to the plate and fulfill that calling. God will bless those efforts, because they are in direct obedience to Him.

As homeschooling moms we will also have ample opportunity to impart the Word to our offspring. We are with them all day long, and ideally it would come naturally to us to talk about God in all that we do. This will make God real to our children, rather than Him appearing to be far-off somewhere. Let our little ones know that the Lord is involved in all areas of your life, and soon they will be involving Him in all areas of their own lives.

Let me just say that we have a great opportunity before us. Use every resource you can to teach your kids about the Lord. Read books, listen to audio programs, use a concordance, create fun games for prayer time and Bible verse memorization, scour the homeschool catalogs to find resources that will bless your family; use any means necessary to impart the Word of God to your child or children! Make that the priority of your homeschool day, and all the rest will be added unto you, just as Jesus promised.

Day Three

Today's lesson is taken from Matthew chapter five, a chapter absolutely full of treasure. You found this chapter of the Bible listed in your suggested daily reading for Week 2, Day 3. Feel free to skim over the entire chapter to refresh your memory if you so choose. Here we find the Sermon on the Mount and the Beatitudes, among the wealth of other teachings from our Lord. While we will look at a portion of this chapter on our final day of study, today I'd like us to look at verses 43-48. Please read them now.

Not only does Jesus tell us to do what seems nearly impossible (love our enemies, pray for our persecutors), He also tells us to do something totally impossible! To be perfect. Please write verse 48 out in the lines below.

_____
_____
_____
_____

As a homeschooling mother of five, I can attest to the fact that I've never felt perfect in the way I deal with my children. Yet I attempt to do all the things Jesus mentioned in verses 43-47. I know I am not the only believer that has ever seriously pondered a portion of God's Word. God is gracious. He promised to give wisdom to anyone who asks it of Him. Please copy the words of James 1:5 below.

_____
_____
_____
_____

Let's pray and ask God to give us the wisdom we need to more fully understand His Word.

Father, how we praise You for Your Word. You have given us all that we need for life and godliness through Your Holy Word. We ask You today to give us Your wisdom and understanding as we seek to learn and grow from Your Word. We thank You that You hear our prayers and answer them. In Your Son's Name we pray, AMEN.

In Matthew 5:48, the Lord tells us to be perfect, as our Father in heaven is perfect. In order to be able to apply this verse to our lives, we need to clarify what it does and does not mean. The word perfect comes from the Greek word teleios (tel-i-os). The second definition (Strong's Greek #5046) means "wanting nothing necessary to completeness". Once we have accepted Christ's death on the cross as payment for our personal sin, and believe that He will raise us to eternal life as He was raised from the dead, then we no longer have want of anything to make us complete. The fourth definition of the Greek word teleios reads this way:

"That which is perfect
    4a) consummate human integrity and virtue
    4b) of men
        4b1) full grown, adult, of full age, mature

So here we see that in regard to God, He is and always has been fully perfect. In regard to His followers, we are to combine human integrity and virtue, and to become full grown and mature in our faith. Suddenly being perfect doesn't seem quite so impossible, does it?

Write out verse 48 again, this time in your own words, incorporating what we've learned about the meaning of the word "perfect".

_____
_____
_____
_____
_____
_____

Now let's look at the word heaven in verse 48. This word can be found in Strong's Concordance as Greek #3772. The word is ouranos (oo-ran-os). The second definition of the word ouranos reads this way: "The region above the side real heavens, the seat of order of things eternal and consummately perfect. Where God dwells and other heavenly beings." Do you recognize a similar word in the definitions of both words? I saw "consummate" in the word teleois, and "consummately" in the word ouranos.

Please look up consummate in a dictionary and write the definition below.

_____
_____
_____
_____
_____
_____

The Webster's 1828 Dictionary defines consummate this way: "to finish by completing what was intended; to perfect; to bring or carry to the utmost point or degree." Webster used the following as an example of the word consummate in a sentence. "He had a mind to consummate the happiness of the day." (Tatler)

Entry number 9 of the definition of consummate reads "complete; perfect; carried to the utmost extent or degree." The word consummately has a definition stating, "completely; perfectly." And the word consummating is defined, "completing; accomplishing; perfecting."

I realize that not everyone is a word person, but I most certainly am! Due to the fact that I learn best via the written word, I love this type of Bible exploration. But since not everyone best learns the way I do, I'd like to try and clarify what all these definitions and Greek root words mean for us as homeschoolers.

Here is what I believe this verse says to us based on the study of the root words. Keep in mind that I have written out the actual verse, but added the words in parenthesis based on the original definitions. "But you are to be perfect (or full grown, adult, completing a mix of human integrity and virtue), as your Father in heaven (the seat of order of things eternal, and already completely perfect where the Father dwells) is perfect (wanting nothing necessary to completeness)."

That is my understanding of the meaning of Matthew 5:48 and it is absolutely something that every one of us can do! Can you live as a mature Christian? Can you become full-grown and adult in your faith? Then you are able to fulfill Jesus' directive to be perfect. Since the Father dwells in a realm where eternity is being ordered, a realm where everything is already perfect, and since He needs nothing to be complete, we understand that we cannot attain that type of perfection. All our perfection on the other side of death will be of His doing, not our own. Isn't it a blessing to know that what the Lord is asking of us is simply to grow up in the Word? To grow up to be just like Him! I encourage you to use a concordance and a dictionary in your own Bible study time. Dig into God's Word! Don't assume you'll never understand certain verses or passages; instead, assume He will continue to teach and mature you! Prepare to be blessed as you study His Word!

Day Four

In today's lesson I'd like to look at a few verses that I personally use in my homeschool. I keep them in my planner where I can regularly review them. These three verses are one way I hold myself accountable, a way to remain true to my call as a homeschooling mother.

The first verse is Proverbs 19:8. In the New Living Translation it reads, "To acquire wisdom is to love oneself; people who cherish understanding will prosper". Your translation may read a bit differently, but the core meaning is still the same. Not only do I wish to impart wisdom and understanding to my five children, I also want to grow in my own wisdom and understanding. But what is wisdom? Please look up the word wisdom in a dictionary and write the definition below.

_____
_____
_____
_____
_____

According to Dr. Henrietta C. Mears, in her book What the Bible Is All About, Bible Handbook, the word wisdom means, "knowledge, understanding, applying knowledge and insights to life situations. Wisdom in the Bible usually refers to a God-given ability, rather than human common sense."

This definition of wisdom falls in line with the words of the Apostle Paul in 1 Corinthians 1:12. Please write that verse on these lines.

_____
_____
_____
_____

When we depend on God's grace instead of our own earthly wisdom, we will truly be able to prosper. Our homes, our marriages, our friendships, our churches, and our homeschools will all benefit as we apply this type of wisdom! Our children will be blessed to strive toward this in their own walk with the Lord.

The next verse I would like to examine is Proverbs 19:20. Please write this verse below.

_____
_____
_____
_____

The NLT says, "Get all the advice and instruction you can, and be wise the rest of your life." This verse does not seem to imply that learning stops when formal education ends. Rather, it teaches us that we all need to continue to learn, seeking out advice and instruction to the end of our days. These words encourage me to continue learning and seeking out godly teaching, as I in turn pass that love of learning on to the next generation.

What does this verse say to you?

_____
_____
_____
_____
_____
_____
_____

My continuing prayer for all who participate in this study is that they will press on to obtain all the advice and instruction that they can, and to acquire wisdom as they live in God's grace.

The last verse we're going to study today is Psalm 101:2b. Please take a moment to look up this verse. The second half of the verse in the NLT reads, "I will lead a life of integrity in my own home." The author of this Psalm was King David, a man well acquainted with the pain that life can bring, as we studied in week 5. He was certainly not immune to the sin nature of man. Yet he says in this Psalm that he would lead a life of integrity in his own home. How was he able to do that? How can we learn to do that?

The bad news is, it's not easy to lead a life of integrity in our homes. The good news is that if it were easy, we wouldn't depend so dearly upon the Lord to accomplish it. Let's be honest, any time we spend leaning upon the Lord in unceasing measure is time well spent, no matter how trying the situation may be.

I'd like you to return to your dictionary to look up the word integrity.

Integrity:

_____

_____

The Noah Webster's 1828 American Dictionary of the English Language defines integrity in this way.

1. "Wholeness; entireness; unbroken state.
2. "The entire, unimpaired state of any thing, particularly of the mind; moral soundness or purity; incorruptness; uprightness; honesty
3. "Purity"

What I glean from this verse after studying the definitions of the word integrity is that my goal in my home life ought to be wholeness, moral soundness and purity, honesty, and uprightness. Once again, we are faced with a task that seems impossible. But take heart, for as Jesus said, "Humanly speaking, it is impossible. But with God everything is possible". (See Matthew 19:26)

We seem to have come full circle over these six weeks in one regard. We began this Bible study by confirming that there isn't anything in our lives that is beyond the Lord God. We're ending it on the same note. Praise God Almighty, for everything is possible with Him!

Day Five

We've reached the final day in our short homeschool Bible study. Have we changed at all? I certainly hope so. Have we learned some ways to cope with our homeschool struggles? I pray that we have.

As I finish writing this study, I want to share about my family's current situation. My husband is an officer in the National Guard, and is currently in command of a unit working in Louisiana following the hurricanes Katrina and Rita. Just a few days before he left for this mission, we stood and said goodbye to yet another comrade preparing to leave for Iraq. My husband's closest friend in the military is halfway through his second tour in Iraq, while his wife waits at home with their baby and another child on the way. Nine months ago my husband left his full-time civilian job and began leaving for work wearing a green uniform rather than a shirt and tie. Neither of us has any idea when this season of our lives may end or where this road may lead us. I suspect the Lord has had me working on this study for a variety of reasons, but I believe He knew I would need to be firmly rooted in His Word during this season of my life. How do I deal with my day-to-day problems without my spouse to lean on? How can I sleep at night without worrying intensely about my husband? Or about our friends deployed overseas? I lean heavily upon my Savior, and on the fellow Christians He has lovingly placed in my life.

My work as a homeschooler has not ceased while my husband is away. My time with my children is still limited. I am still obligated by God to use each day to the fullest in order to influence this world for His glory. My strength comes from Him, and any fruit in my life is for His praise.

Please read Matthew 5:13-16. According to Jesus, what are we supposed to be to the world?

_____

_____

Salt and light. Now please turn to Isaiah 54:13. What does this verse say?

_____

_____

_____

I am continuing to believe that God will work out Isaiah 54:13 in my life and my children's lives. He will enable me to teach them, yes, but He will also teach them Himself, and He promises that their prosperity will be great. I desire for my children to prosper in the Lord. While God always provides for us as His children, and often blesses His children financially, I want this verse to have spiritual applications for my offspring.

Please list some ways in which you desire your children to prosper.

_____
_____
_____
_____
_____
_____

Our children will fully prosper only if they take what God has taught them and refuse to hide it. Combining our learning with love, and continuing on as salt and light is a part of our calling as homeschoolers. God wants the world to be changed through us. So let's allow God to teach us, be salt and light to those around us, and expect God to bless us!

The last few verses we're going to look at are found in Psalm 32. Although I want you to read these verses in your own Bible, I would like to focus on them from the New Living Translation. Please read verses 8 and 9 below, and then feel free to read them in your Bible.

The Lord says, "I will guide you along the best pathway, I will advise you and watch over you. Do not be like a senseless horse or mule that needs a bit and bridle to keep it under control." (NLT)

These verses speak volumes to me regarding God's love and care. He watches over every detail of our lives. Nothing gets past Him unnoticed! He desires for us to walk with Him in wide open spaces, with times of refreshing and joy. He also knows that sometimes we have to be led with a bit and bridle – although it's uncomfortable, it gets us where we need to be. Which lifestyle would you prefer? Which do you want for your children?

I want to encourage you to redouble your efforts as you homeschool – not by your own strength but by fully trusting in the Lord. Continue on this path that God has called you to. And be joy filled that He so graciously allows us to take part in His work on earth! He will guide you along the best pathway, but He desires to lead you without the bit and bridle.

In closing, I would like to encourage you to memorize Psalm 32:8-9 as your final memory work assignment. Thank you for studying God's Word with me. What a privilege it is to be a part of this awesome homeschool adventure with so many women who deeply love the Lord! May He bless you a hundred fold in all you do for His glory.

Notes

All verses quoted from the New Living Translation unless otherwise noted. (Life Application Study Bible, New Living Translation, copyright 1996)

All Greek and Hebrew references from the Strong's Exhaustive Concordance King James Version online at www.lifeway.com unless otherwise noted

All word definitions taken from the American Dictionary of the English Language, Noah Webster, 1828, Facsimile First Edition unless otherwise noted

Week One, Day Four

Ephesians 3:20 quoted from the Young's Literal Translation, the New King James Version, the New American Standard Bible, the King James Bible, and the Holman Christian Standard Bible.

Week Three, Day Three

Joshua 5:12 quoted from the King James Version, and the Holman Christian Standard Bible

Week Three, Day Four

Psalm 15:4 and Psalm 15:5b quoted from the King James Version

Week Five, Day Four

I Corinthians 13:2b quoted from the King James Version

Week Six, Day Four

Quote taken from the book "What the Bible is All About, Bible Handbook, NIV Edition, by Henrietta C. Mears (copyright 1998)

Weekly Memory Verses

Week One - Ephesians 3:12

Week Two - Ephesians 3:20

Week Three - Psalm 71:18b

Week Four - Isaiah 38:19

Week Five - Psalm 32:8

    Above I have listed the notations for the verses rather than the verses in their entirety. You may prefer to memorize them in the version you most frequently read. I have left that for your preference. If you would like to memorize them in the NLT, I have listed them below.

    Ephesians 3:12 - "Because of Christ and our faith in him, we can now come fearlessly into God's presence, assured of his glad welcome."

    Ephesians 3:20 - "Now glory be to God! By his mighty power at work within us, he is able to accomplish infinitely more than we would ever dare to ask or hope."

    Psalm 71:18b - "Let me proclaim your power to this new generation, your mighty miracles to all who come after me."

Isaiah 38:19 - "Only the living can praise you as I do today. Each generation can make known your faithfulness to the next."

Psalm 32:8 - "The Lord says, ' I will guide you along the best pathway for your life. I will advise you and watch over you.' "

Daily Bible Reading

Week One

    Day One - Psalm 91

    Day Two - Jeremiah 17

    Day Three - Psalm 81

    Day Four - Ephesians 3

    Day Five - Mark 13

Week Two

    Day One - Romans 1, Romans 2

    Day Two - Psalm 51

    Day Three - Matthew 5

    Day Four - Psalm 71

    Day Five - Mark 5

Week Three

Day One - Joshua 5

Day Two - Psalm 103

Day Three - Joshua 1

Day Four - Psalm 15

Day Five - Luke 19

Week Four

Day One - Proverbs 29

Day Two - Acts 22

Day Three - 2 Samuel 15

Day Four - Psalm 18

Day Five - 2 Samuel 16

Week Five

Day One - Isaiah 38

Day Two - Matthew 18

Day Three - 1 Corinthians 12

Day Four - 1 Corinthians 13

Day Five - 2 Kings 2

Week Six

Day One - Ecclesiastes 10, Matthew 7

Day Two - Psalm 78

Day Three - James 1

Day Four - John 15

Day Five - Isaiah 54, Psalm 32

Recommended Reading List

On This Day by Robert J. Morgan, Thomas Nelson Publishers, copyright 1997

Discover Your Child's Gifts by Don and Katie Fortune, Chosen Books, copyright 1989

The Ultimate Guide to Homeschooling by Debra Bell, Tommy Nelson, copyright 1997, 2000

Things We Wish We'd Known compiled and edited by Bill and Diana Waring, Emerald Books, copyright 1999

The Underground History of American Education by John Taylor Gatto (Former New York State & New York City Teacher of the Year), The Oxford Village Press, copyright 2000/2001

What the Bible Is All About Bible Handbook by Henrietta C. Mears, Regal Books, copyright 1998

Praying God's Word by Beth Moore, Broadman & Holman Publishers, copyright 2000

A Garden Patch of Reproducible Homeschooling Planning & Educational Worksheets by Debora McGregor, copyright 1996, 1999

Growing Little Women by Donna J. Miller and Christine Yount, Moody Press, copyright 2000

When Your Child Is 6 to 12 by John M. Drescher, Good Books, copyright 1993

A Mom Just Like You by Vickie Farris and Jayme Farris Metzgar, Broadman & Holman Publishers, copyright 2000, 2002

Life Skills for Kids by Christine M. Field, Shaw, copyright 2000

Help for the Harried Homeschooler by Christine M. Field, Shaw Books, copyright 2002

Homeschooling Mother's Bible Study Re-Order Form

Name:
_____

Address:
_____

City, State, Zip:
_____

Email:
_____

Number of Copies Requested: _____   Amount Enclosed: _____

Cost per study $15.00, shipping included.

Please enclose payment with this form and mail to:
Jan Burt
5021 Pembrook Court
Wichita, KS 67220

For questions or further information, please email janburt@cox.net

----

Please feel free to duplicate this page in order for others to order this study. If you have been blessed by this look into God's Word, I would greatly appreciate you sharing it with your fellow homeschoolers. As I hope to write further studies aimed at encouraging home educating families, you may send me your contact information and I will notify when more studies become available.

Made in the USA
Lexington, KY
29 December 2017